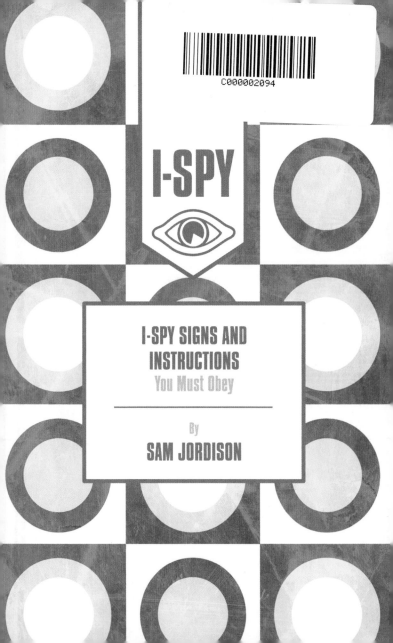

I-SPY

I-SPY SIGNS AND INSTRUCTIONS
You Must Obey

By

SAM JORDISON

HarperCollins*Publishers*
1 London Bridge Street
London SE1 9GF

www.harpercollins.co.uk

First published by HarperCollins*Publishers* 2016

10 9 8 7 6 5 4 3 2

© Sam Jordison 2016
Designed by Alexandra Allden © HarperCollins*Publishers* 2016

Sam Jordison asserts the moral right to be identified as
the author of this work

A catalogue record of this book is available from the
British Library

ISBN 978-0-00-822069-3

Printed and bound in Spain

MIX
Paper from
responsible sources
FSC C007454

FSC™ is a non-profit international organisation established to promote the
responsible management of the world's forests. Products carrying the FSC
label are independently certified to assure consumers that they come from
forests that are managed to meet the social, economic and ecological needs
of present and future generations, and other controlled sources.

Find out more about HarperCollins and the environment at
www.harpercollins.co.uk/green

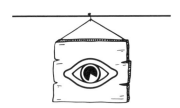

The I-SPY concept is simple. It's like the 'I spy with my little eye' game, only instead of all the tedious stuff about 'something beginning with', there are pictures and descriptions and genuine opportunities to use your sleuthing skills to discover interesting things. And laugh at them. It will greatly improve your thus far ignorant life.

Britain is simply brimming with officious signs. Instructions are everywhere. It's fun to note down as many different ones as you can. It's not fun to defy them, however. Because then people will tut at you – and this is worse than death.

This book provides a useful guide to the signs you are likely to see strategically placed around the UK. It teaches us that it's not only necessary to obey orders, but enjoyable too. It makes good spies of us all!

You earn a score every time you spot something pictured in the I-SPY books. It's great fun to add up your scores and know that you're doing better than your friends and family.

When your score totals over 250, you're allowed to call yourself an I-SPY Stalwart, second-class honours.

When your score totals over 500, you can write to me, Chief I-SPY, and apply for a special badge.

If you score less than 250, you're a failure and should probably report yourself to the police.

Chief I-SPY, LONDON

No Ball Games

This is one of the easiest signs to spot around the streets and towns of the UK. You will see it everywhere as it's important that no one has any fun whatsoever with balls. It's a small leap from playing in the street to joining a gang or left-wing political pressure group, and all communal activities should therefore be discouraged.

The sign pictured is particularly useful because it also tells Welsh people how to behave.

I-SPYed on .... Score
at .... (20)

Sandwich Board

Some very decent and pious citizens have taken it upon themselves to issue instructions and reinforce the all-important status quo even as they walk around.

(For your own safety, we advise you not to engage these people in conversation or otherwise approach them.)

I-SPYed on .... **Score**

at .... (**20**)

Extreme No Parking Sign

For some people, the instruction 'no parking' isn't enough. There is clearly some part of the word 'no' that they don't understand. They have to be dealt with. There's no point being passive-aggressive in these circumstances. We must be entirely aggressive. Naked, violent threats are clearly the best and most effective medicine, and that's why it's nice to see so many of these signs scattered across our island home.

I-SPYed on .... Score

at .... (20)

See a car parked in the no-parking zone and report it to the proper authorities for 30 extra points.

I-SPYed on .... Score

at .... (30)

Don't even think about parking

HERE

Beware of Buses

Even the most innocuous-seeming objects can be full of
threat and hidden danger. After nightfall, buses roam the
streets looking for innocent citizens to pick up and carry
far from home and safety.

I-SPYed on .... Score

at .... (40)

No Skateboarding or Similar Activities

Skateboarding is fun and something that young people like to do. Which is why it is quite correct that it should be forbidden in public. All good citizens will delight to see these signs.

I-SPYed on.. Score

at .... (20)

Similar activities include rollerblading, smoking drugs, smiling and public kissing. Score 10 bonus points for each one of these that you see. And 20 for each one you report to the proper authorities.

I-SPYed on.. Score

at .... (30)

SKATEBOARDING
PROHIBITED

Useful Instructions for Cyclists

Cyclists! You may think you are reducing traffic, cutting down pollution, getting fit and having fun in the process, but actually, you are the enemy. You challenge the status quo, you may well be left wing and you certainly deserve to be punished. This kind of cycle-lane instruction is here to ensure that you don't develop any foolish notions about actually getting anywhere. Know your place!

I-SPYed on .... **Score**

at .... (30)

There are lovely bonus points up for grabs if you see a cyclist coming a cropper thanks to a cycle lane's clever design.

I-SPYed on .... **Score**

at .... (30)

Philosophical Graffiti

Do NOT try to answer this question! Or any other questions written on walls by people who don't represent the correct authorities. Especially if they're poorly punctuated. Collect your points and move on.

I-SPYed on .... Score

at .... (30)

Harmful Innuendo

You might think signs like this one are funny,
but they aren't.

I-SPYed on .... **Score**

at .... (**10**)

ST. GREGORYS
BACK ALLEY

Lewd Graffiti

This isn't funny either. And, most probably, very easy to factually disprove. It's an important lesson in why we must only pay attention to signs erected by respectable government organisations.

I-SPYed on .... **Score**

at .... **(10)**

Newbury District Council

Deceptive Sign

Most signs are designed for the benefit of right-thinking people and have the good of society in mind. But, sadly, this is not always the case. Disruptive elements have erected a number of misleading and otherwise counter-productive signs. This sign, for instance, is in Wrexham, where there has been no hope since 1979.

I-SPYed on .... **Score**

at .... (**40**)

Stop Children Sign

Some people contend that there are good arguments for the existence of children, but I'm afraid I just can't think what they might be. Seriously, enough is enough. It's time we took to the streets and made our case against these noisy, snot-nosed, me-me-me machines. Some brave ladies and gentlemen even take their protest to the school gates, carrying signs like the one pictured. They're easily spotted in the early morning and afternoon, and we must only commend them.

I-SPYed on .... Score

at 20

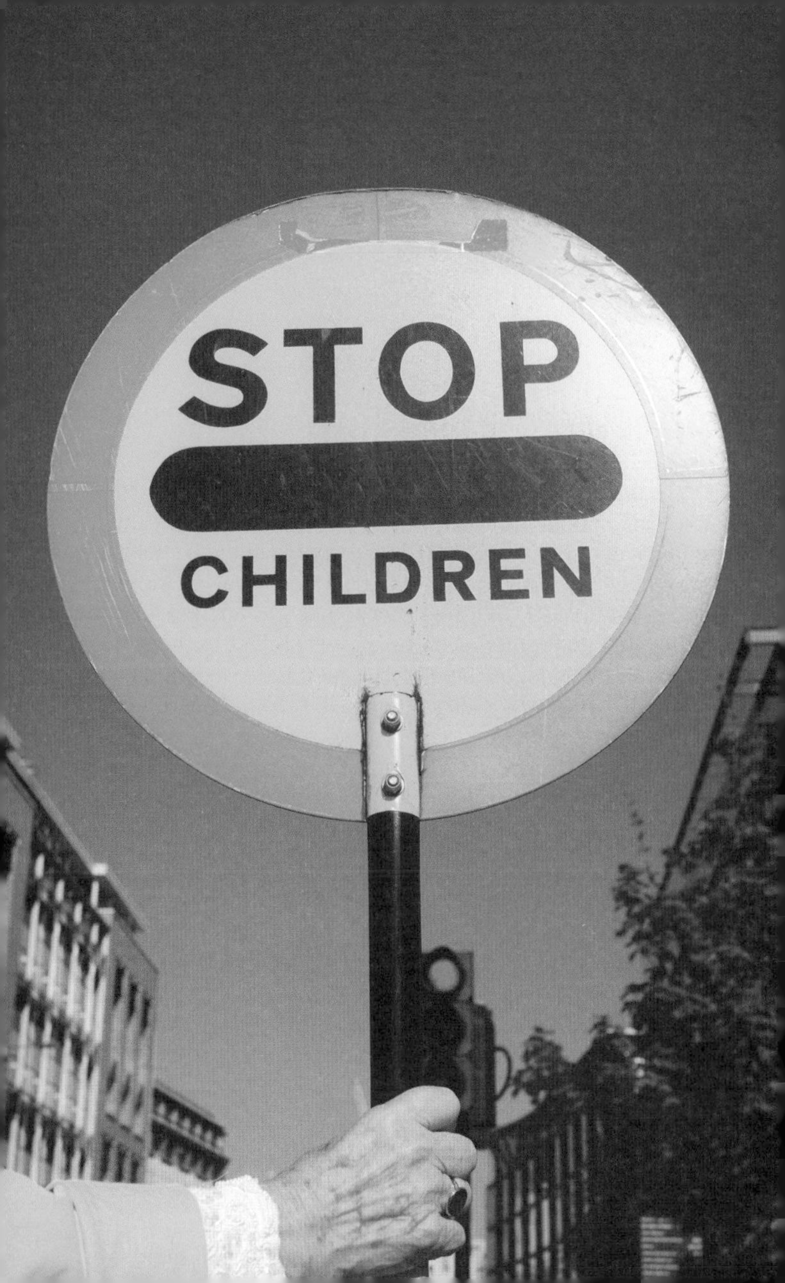
STOP
CHILDREN

Instructions for the Use of Toilet Facilities

These signs provide a useful reminder that men are disgusting. They must be regularly told where they can and can't point their prangs. There's a time and a place for everything and it generally isn't out on the street.

I-SPYed on... Score

at .... ⑳

WORKMEN:

You are welcome to use this toilet but remember this is <u>NOT</u> an onsite toilet and is used by the general public.

<u>PLEASE:</u> Lift the seat and flush after use.

<u>THANKS.</u>

PLEASE USE
TOILETS
PROVIDED

Troublingly Unspecific Sign

I'm not sure where to draw the line on this. Does it
include toilet roll? Have you – and I'm sorry for asking
this – have you, strictly speaking, actually eaten the
things that come out of your unmentionable regions?
Look. It's probably best that you don't use this toilet
at all. Just note down your I-SPY points, hold in what
you've got to hold in and walk on. Some challenges
just aren't worth the candle.

I-SPYed on .... **Score**

at .... **(40)**

Security Cameras

The State is always watching you. But you can watch it back! And get some lovely I-SPY points in the process.

I-SPYed on... **Score**

at .... ⑩

YOU ARE
BEING
VIDEOTAPED
SMILE!

Tractor-related signage

If you see a sign about a tractor, it means you're to be congratulated because you've escaped the big, bad city and made it to safer, saner regions. Places like Norfolk, where the closest they get to thug life is when someone parks their farm machinery on double yellow lines.

But! As anyone who has been stuck behind one on the A17 will know, tractors just don't go slowly enough. Luckily our friends in the police have erected useful signs to prevent any unfortunate accidents that might otherwise be caused – such as anyone actually arriving anywhere on time.

I-SPYed on .... Score

at .... (50)

POLICE NOTICE

Tractors: please slow down

Help to make our communities safer...

Contact your
Safer Neighbourhood Team on
01202 / 01305 22 22 22

www.**dorset**.police.uk

Useful Bulletins from the Mainstream Media

Be alert for non-permanent signs and warnings provided by members of the Fourth Estate. The information they contain can be important and enriching, and give you valuable insight into the area in which you are conducting your spying operations.

I-SPYed on .... **Score**

at .... (**20**)

CROYDON ADVERTISER
making local matter more
this is croydon today.co.uk
WOMAN DIED EATING SUNDAY ROAST
CROYDON ADVERTISER
making local matter more
this is croydon today.co.uk

Weak-minded Sign

Sometimes hippies write signs. Ignore them!

I-SPYed on .... **Score**

at .... (10)

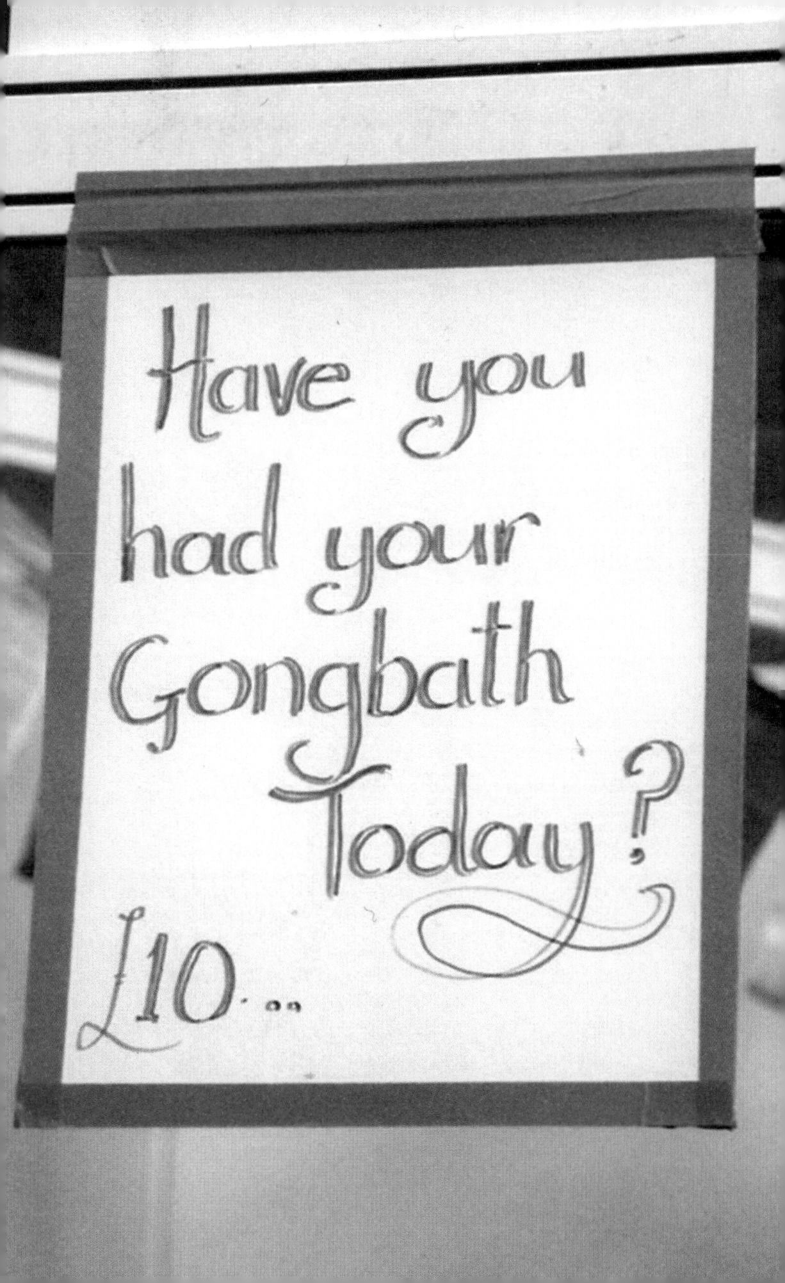
Have you
had your
Gongbath
Today?
£10...

Brutally Real Sign

I hate to be the bringer of bad news, but life is hard.
Sometimes ships sink. Sometimes bolts of electricity
come down from the sky and fry people's brains.
Sometimes pinstripe, eggburp mini-Hitlers will try to
steal your European citizenship. Be vigilant. Obey all
such signs and award yourself some lovely I-SPY points
if you see one. But don't say you weren't warned when
things don't quite work out.

I-SPYed on .... **Score**

at .... (30)

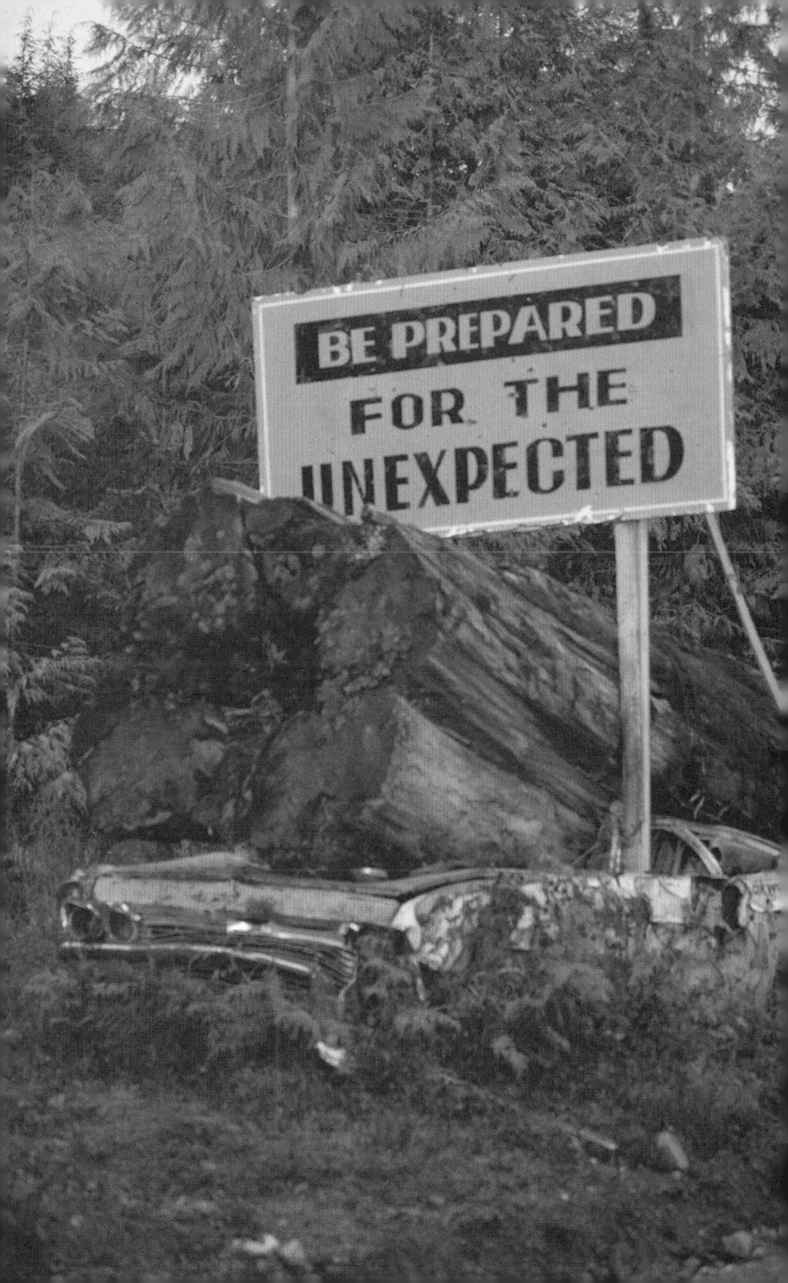
BE PREPARED
FOR THE
UNEXPECTED

'Humorously' Altered Sign

Some people think they're funny and try to alter official signs to subvert their important messages. These people aren't as amusing as they think. And they are going to get into trouble.

I-SPYed on .... **Score**

at .... (**20**)

Return the sign to its original pure state and Chief I-Spy will be delighted to grant you an extra 40 points.

I-SPYed on .... **Score**

at .... (**40**)

STOP
Worrying

Home-made Sign

Just because you aren't in a position of authority, don't think that you can't tell other people what to do. A good I-SPYer should always be prepared to both lay down and enforce the law. If, like all good citizens, you own your own property, you can erect nearly any kind of sign you like on it. Many other good citizens have done so and you can award yourself points for seeing them.

I-SPYed on .... Score

at .... (20)

Testing Sign

Why would you want to throw stones at a sign? What could possibly happen if you did? Who would see you anyway, and what harm would it do? Go on. Just a little stone. It won't hurt. There's no one around...

MY GOD! STOP IMMEDIATELY! Remember what happened in the Garden of Eden! Remember what happens to anyone who disobeys orders.

I-SPYed on... Score

at .... **(20)**

Did you manage not to throw stones at the sign? Award yourself 20 bonus points.

I-SPYed on... Score

at .... **(20)**

Are you actually lying about not throwing stones? Deduct 50 points.

I-SPYed on... Score

at .... **(-50)**

PLEASE
DO NOT THROW
ROCKS
AT THIS SIGN

Long Sign

This sign is impressively comprehensive. The sign writer has made excellent use of the space allotted to him* to cover numerous important eventualities. The prohibition against glasses is perhaps unfair on those with visual problems – but so is life. It will toughen them up.

All good citizens will enjoy and benefit from obeying this sign's instructions to the letter. Usefully, it even tells your dogs what to do. Too often, dogs operate under the belief that instructions do not apply to them – and they must be corrected on this.

*Of course it's a him! Do you think a woman would write a sign like this?

I-SPYed on .... Score

at .... (30)

VEHICLES PROHIBITED
—— NO CYCLES ——
RIDDEN OR OTHERWISE · WITHOUT A PERMIT

ALL HORSES MUST DISPLAY A
CURRENT RIDING PERMIT DISC
AND RIDERS ARE REQUESTED
TO KEEP OFF ANY MOWN GRASS

NO ROLLERBLADING

VISITORS ARE WARNED THAT
MANY·OF THE TREES ARE OLD
AND LIABLE TO SHED THEIR
BRANCHES AT ANYTIME

DOGS MUST NOT BE ALLOWED
TO FOUL MOWN GRASS AND
ARE TO BE KEPT UNDER
STRICT CONTROL OR ON LEADS

GLASSES MUST NOT BE TAKEN
INTO THE LONG WALK

Ultimate Sign

This is the holy grail for keen I-SPYers! It is the most instructive sign in the UK. Its creators are even aware of the threat posed by buskers. It's beautiful. It's carefully maintained in a secret underground location.

I-SPYed on .... **Score**

at .... (250)

If you obey every single instruction on this sign, for ever, award yourself an extra 400 points.

I-SPYed on .... **Score**

at .... (400)

NO CYCLING
BUSKING
ANIMAL FOULING
LITTERING
LOITERING
SKATEBOARDING
SKATING
SPITTING

DOGS TO BE KEPT ON LEADS
KEEP LEFT

Honourable Rank of
NEW SPY

—

Awarded to

....

from

....

....

(FULL NAME AND ADDRESS HERE)

has become an acceptable citizen. This person has
demonstrated vigilance and diligence and earned
the Honourable Rank of New Spy.

First-class Honours
1000 POINTS - EXTRA MERIT

NOW ENCOURAGE YOUR FRIENDS AND NEIGHBOURS TO JOIN IN. OR ELSE.